INSIGHTS
Forgiveness

INSIGHTS

Forgiveness

What the Bible Tells Us about Christian Forgiveness

WILLIAM BARCLAY

SAINT ANDREW PRESS
Edinburgh

First published in 2012 by
SAINT ANDREW PRESS
121 George Street
Edinburgh EH2 4YN

ISBN 978 0 7152 0934 9

British Library Cataloguing in Publication Date
A catalogue record for this book is available from the British Library.

It is the publisher's policy to only use papers that are natural and
recyclable and that have been manufactured from timber grown
in renewable, properly managed forests. All of the manufacturing
processes of the papers are expected to conform to the environmental
regulations of the country of origin.

Typeset by Waverley Typesetters, Warham, Norfolk
Printed and bound by CPI Group (UK) Ltd, Croydon CR0 4YY

Contents

Foreword

One wintry evening I was called to the old Royal Infirmary of Edinburgh because a Norwegian student who attended our church had been hurt in a traffic accident. I soon discovered how grave the accident had been.

A man, having had his driving licence removed, under the influence of alcohol, driving a stolen car, had crashed into parked cars on a steep city street. Nils had been trapped between two such cars. By the time I reached the infirmary, the left leg had been amputated above the knee. The fight to save the right leg was on.

I knelt on the floor by his bedside to hear his whispered words. Tears of rage and anguish rolled down my face. He looked at me through mists of medication and said, 'Do not weep for me. I forgive him.' 'I can't forgive him,' I was thinking savagely. And my look betrayed me. 'The Lord Jesus has forgiven me *and him*. If Jesus has forgiven me how can I not forgive him?' His words were blurred as he dipped in and out of consciousness, but the meaning was plain. 'Your Mum and Dad are coming,' I whispered. 'They are on the plane now. You will see them in the morning.' He smiled and closed his eyes, drifting into sedated sleep. Nils embodied what William Barclay writes about in this *Insight* on Forgiveness.

How can we forgive others?

Why do we need forgiveness?

How often must we forgive?

What is the cost of forgiveness?

Why is forgiving so hard for most of us?

Why is forgiving others a healing experience for us?

Can human love have a redeeming quality that brings us forgiveness?

Barclay, steeped in classical languages and English literature, takes us through a number of New Testament passages with his characteristic detailed examination of the meanings of the Greek and the implications for the first hearers and for us. These studies are still both immediate and relevant. They would make an excellent basis for individual devotion or for house group study. It may be about fifty years since Barclay wrote these words. The world is fifty years older in war, terrorism, broken relationships, lack of honour, exploitation, and misery. It would be good to explore in a study group what forgiveness means in world politics, in acts of terror, in ecumenical relationships, in industry, local community and in families, as well as individually. More than ever we need to know the grace of Jesus Christ and rejoice in forgiving love.

What happened to young Nils? Despite the best efforts of the medical profession he lost the second leg below the knee. He has, in his own words, 'two tin legs', the left painted red and the right painted green – to honour the shipping tradition into which he was born. He completed his degree at Heriot-Watt University without missing a year. He is a successful businessman in Oslo. He sails and skis and is in a loving and permanent relationship. He does much work for the charity which supports the limbless in his native Norway. Recently he was awarded an honorary degree from his *alma mater.* Did he have days of pain and difficulty? Of course he did and still does. But he was never eaten by bitterness or blame or rancour. He lived and lives in the forgiveness of Christ.

This *Insight* on Forgiveness helps us all to do just that.

MARGARET R. FORRESTER

Publisher's Introduction

⌜One of the most familiar statements about forgiveness comes from the Lord's Prayer where we are told to forgive as we have been forgiven.⌟ This is not something altogether easy to understand or to practice, particularly as it means engaging with the concept of sin. But for William Barclay this statement is fundamental to Jesus' teaching. He explains in a clear and engaging way the idea of sin and ⌜the need for recognition of our faults in order to appreciate the forgiveness that God offers.⌟ In turn we must learn to understand before condemning, to forget and put things well and truly in the past, and also to love, so that we too can offer the forgiveness that we seek for ourselves.

The idea that our forgiveness of one another and God's forgiveness of us cannot be separated is one that runs through the New Testament. Jesus taught his disciples about the importance of genuine forgiveness. We hear about the servant who was forgiven a great debt, and about the sinful woman whose anointing of Jesus brought her forgiveness. The teaching of the early church, found in the letters of Paul and John and James also shows that compassion, understanding and recognition of our own faults make it possible to accept God's freely given forgiveness. The extracts found in this book show how Jesus' message stated so clearly in his words from the cross, 'Father, forgive them', also became central to the teaching of his followers. Jesus himself brought God's forgiveness to all.

In the final example, Barclay sheds light on one of the most difficult passages in the Gospels where we are told that there is one sin that cannot be forgiven, the sin described as that against the Holy Spirit. Here he explains that forgiveness is in our own hands. Those who do not recognize their shortcomings feel no need for forgiveness and so it cannot be given. The message is ultimately the same as in the other passages. If we recognize our failings God freely forgives and we must do the same for one another.

The examples of teaching about forgiveness found here in *Insights: Forgiveness* all have a wider context, which you can find in Barclay's *New Daily Study Bible* series. Each book of the New Testament has its own writer, style of writing, historical background, original readership and so on. In reading about these, we can add to our understanding of the Bible. We hope you will be inspired to learn more about the New Testament through William Barclay's classic books. A list of them can be found at the end of this book.

Forgiveness human and divine

Matthew 6:12, 14–15

> *Forgive us our debts as we forgive our debtors ... For, if you*
> *forgive men their trespasses, your heavenly Father will forgive*
> *you too; but if you do not forgive men their trespasses, neither*
> *will your Father forgive your trespasses.*

BEFORE we can honestly pray this petition of the Lord's Prayer,
we must realize that we need to pray it. That is to say, before
we can pray this petition we must have a sense of sin. Sin is
not nowadays a popular word. Men and women rather resent
being called, or treated as, hell-deserving sinners.

The trouble is that most people have a wrong conception
of sin. They would readily agree that the burglar, the
drunkard, the murderer, the adulterer and the foul-mouthed
person are sinners. But they themselves are guilty of none
of these sins; they live decent, ordinary, respectable lives,
and have never even been in danger of appearing in court,
or going to prison, or achieving some notoriety in the
newspapers. They therefore feel that sin has nothing to do
with them.

The New Testament uses five different words for *sin*.

(1) The most common word is *hamartia*. This was
originally a shooting word and means *a missing of the target*.
To fail to hit the target was *hamartia*. Therefore *sin is the failure
to be what we might have been and could have been*.

The nineteenth-century writer Charles Lamb has a picture of a man named Samuel le Grice. Le Grice was a brilliant youth who never fulfilled his promise. Lamb says that there were three stages in his career. There was a time when people said: 'He will do something.' There was a time when people said: 'He could do something if he would.' There was a time when people said: 'He might have done something, if he had liked.' The poet Edwin Muir writes in his *Autobiography*: 'After a certain age all of us, good and bad, are grief-stricken because of powers within us which have never been realized: because, in other words, we are not what we should be.'

That precisely is *hamartia*; and that is precisely the situation in which we are all involved. Are we as good husbands or wives as we could be? Are we as good sons or daughters as we could be? Are we as good workers or employers as we could be? Can any one of us dare to claim that we are all we might have been, and have done all we could have done? When we realize that sin means the failure to hit the target, the failure to be all that we might have been and could have been, then it is clear that every one of us is a sinner.

(2) The second word for sin is *parabasis*, which literally means *a stepping across. Sin is the stepping across the line which is drawn between right and wrong.*

Do we always stay on the right side of the line which divides honesty and dishonesty? Is there never any such thing as a petty dishonesty in our lives?

Do we always stay on the right side of the line which divides truth and falsehood? Do we never, by word or by silence, twist or evade or distort the truth?

Do we always stay on the right side of the line which divides kindness and courtesy from selfishness and harshness? Is there never an unkind action or a discourteous word in our lives?

When we think of it in this way, there can be none who can claim always to have remained on the right side of the dividing line.

(3) The third word for sin is *paraptōma*, which means *a slipping across*. It is the kind of slip which someone might make on a slippery or an icy road. It is not so deliberate as *parabasis*. Again and again, we speak of words 'slipping out'; again and again, we are swept away by some impulse or passion which has momentarily gained control of us and which has made us lose our self-control. The best of us can slip into sin when for the moment we are off our guard.

(4) The fourth word for sin is *anomia*, which means *lawlessness*. *Anomia* is the sin of the person who knows the right, and who yet does the wrong; the sin of the one who knows the law, and who yet breaks the law. The first of all the human instincts is the instinct to do what we like; and therefore there come into many people's lives times when they wish to kick over the traces and to defy the law, and to do or to take the forbidden thing. In 'Mandalay', Rudyard Kipling makes the old soldier say:

> *Ship me somewheres east of Suez, where the best is like the worst,*
> *Where there aren't no Ten Commandments, an' a man can raise a thirst.*

Even if there are some who can say that they have never broken any of the Ten Commandments, there are none who can say that they have never wished to break any of them.

(5) The fifth word for sin is the word *opheilēma*, which is the word used in the body of the Lord's Prayer; and *opheilēma* means *a debt*. It means *a failure to pay that which is due*, a failure in duty. None of us could ever dare to claim that we have perfectly fulfilled our duty to other people and to God: such perfection does not exist in this world.

So, when we come to see what sin really is, we come to see that it is a universal disease in which we are all involved. Outward respectability in the sight of others and inward sinfulness in the sight of God may well go hand in hand. This, in fact, is a petition of the Lord's Prayer which we all need to pray.

Not only do we need to realize that we need to pray this petition of the Lord's Prayer; we also need to realize what we are doing when we pray it. Of all the petitions of the Lord's Prayer, this is the most frightening.

'Forgive us our debts as we forgive our debtors.' The literal meaning is: 'Forgive us our sins *in proportion as* we forgive those who have sinned against us.' In verses 14 and 15, Jesus says in the plainest possible language that if we forgive others, God will forgive us; but if we refuse to forgive others, God will refuse to forgive us. It is, therefore, quite clear that if we pray this petition with an unhealed breach, an unsettled quarrel in our lives, we are asking God *not* to forgive us.

If we say: 'I will never forgive so-and-so for what he or she has done to me,' if we say: 'I will never forget what so-and-so did to me,' and then go and take this petition on our lips, we are quite deliberately asking God not to forgive us.

As someone has put it: 'Forgiveness, like peace, is one and indivisible.' Human forgiveness and divine forgiveness are inextricably intertwined. Our forgiveness of one another and God's forgiveness of us cannot be separated; they are inter-linked and interdependent. If we remembered what we are doing when we take this petition on our lips, there would be times when we would not dare to pray it.

When Robert Louis Stevenson lived in the South Sea Islands, he always used to conduct family worship in the mornings for his household. It always concluded with the Lord's Prayer. One morning, in the middle of the Lord's Prayer, he rose from his knees and left the room. His health was always precarious, and his wife followed him thinking that he was ill. 'Is there anything wrong?' she said. 'Only this,' said Stevenson. 'I am not fit to pray the Lord's Prayer today.' None of us is fit to pray the Lord's Prayer so long as the unforgiving spirit holds sway within our hearts. If we have not put things right with our neighbours, we cannot put things right with God.

If we are to have this Christian forgiveness in our lives, three things are necessary.

(1) We must learn *to understand*. There is always a reason why people do things. If they are boorish and impolite and bad-tempered, maybe they are worried or in pain. If they treat us with suspicion and dislike, maybe they have misunderstood, or have been misinformed about something we have said or done. Maybe they are victims of their own environment or their own heredity. Maybe they find life difficult, and human relations are a problem for them. Forgiveness would be very much easier for us if we tried to understand before we allowed ourselves to condemn.

(2) We must learn *to forget*. As long as we brood upon a snub or an insult, there is no hope that we will forgive. We so often say: 'I can't forget what so-and-so did to me,' or: 'I will never forget how I was treated by such-and-such a person or in such-and-such a place.' These are dangerous sayings, because we can in the end make it humanly impossible for us to forget. We can print the memory indelibly upon our minds.

The famous Scottish man of letters, Andrew Lang, once wrote and published a very kind review of a book by a young man. The young man repaid him with a bitter and insulting attack. About three years later, Andrew Lang was staying with Robert Bridges, the Poet Laureate. Bridges saw Lang reading a certain book. 'Why,' he said, 'that's another book by that ungrateful young cub who behaved so shamefully to you.' To his astonishment, he found that Andrew Lang's mind was a blank on the whole affair. He had completely forgotten the bitter and insulting attack. To forgive, said Bridges, was the sign of greatness, but to forget was sublime. Nothing but the cleansing spirit of Christ can take from these memories of ours the old bitterness that we must forget.

(3) We must learn *to love*. Christian love, *agapē*, is that unconquerable benevolence, that undefeatable goodwill, which will never seek anything but the highest good of others, no matter what they do to us, and no matter how they treat us. That love can come to us only when Christ, who is that love, comes to dwell within our hearts – and he cannot come unless we invite him.

To be forgiven we must forgive, and that is a condition of forgiveness which only the power of Christ can enable us to fulfil.

How to forgive

Matthew 18:21–35

Then Peter came and said to him: 'Lord, how often will my brother sin against me, and I forgive him? Up to seven times?' Jesus said to him: 'I tell you not up to seven times, but up to seventy times seven. That is why the kingdom of heaven can be likened to what happened when a king wished to make a reckoning with his servants. When he began to make a reckoning, one debtor was brought to him who owed him 10,000 talents. Since he was quite unable to pay, his master ordered him to be sold, together with his wife and children, and all his possessions, and payment to be made. The servant fell on his face and besought him: "Sir, have patience with me, and I will pay you in full." The master of the servant was moved with compassion, and let him go, and forgave him the debt. When that servant went out, he found one of his fellow servants, who owed him 100 denarii. He caught hold of him and seized him by the throat: "Pay what you owe," he said. The fellow servant fell down and besought him: "Have patience with me, and I will pay you in full." But he refused. Rather, he went away and flung him into prison, until he should pay what was due. So, when his fellow servants saw what had happened, they were very distressed; and they went and informed their master of all that had happened. Then the master summoned him, and said to him: "You wicked servant! I forgave you all that debt when you besought me to do so. Ought you not to have had pity on your fellow servant, as I had pity on you?"

*And his master was angry with him and handed him over to
the torturers, until he should pay all that was due.*

*'Even so shall my heavenly Father do to you, if you do not
each one forgive his brother from your hearts.'*

WE owe a very great deal to the fact that Peter had a quick
tongue. Again and again, he rushed into speech in such a
way that his impetuosity drew from Jesus teaching which is
immortal. On this occasion, Peter thought that he was being
very generous. He asked Jesus how often he ought to forgive
someone, and then answered his own question by suggesting
that he should forgive seven times.

Peter was not without warrant for this suggestion. It was
Rabbinic teaching that a person must forgive another *three*
times. Rabbi Jose ben Hanina said: 'He who begs forgiveness
from his neighbour must not do so more than three times.'
Rabbi Jose ben Jehuda said: 'If a man commits an offence
once, they forgive him; if he commits an offence a second
time, they forgive him; if he commits an offence a third
time, they forgive him; the fourth time they do not forgive.'
The biblical proof that this was correct was taken from
Amos. In the opening chapters of Amos, there is a series of
condemnations on the various nations *for three transgressions
and for four* (1:3, 6, 9, 11, 13; 2:1, 4, 6). From this, it was
deduced that God's forgiveness extends to three offences and
that he visits the sinner with punishment at the fourth. It was
not to be thought that people could be more gracious than
God, so forgiveness was limited to three times.

Peter thought that he was going very far, for he takes the
Rabbinic three times, multiplies it by two, for good measure
adds one, and suggests, with eager self-satisfaction, that it will

be enough if he forgives seven times. Peter expected to be warmly commended; but Jesus' answer was that the Christian must forgive seventy times seven. In other words, there is no reckonable limit to forgiveness.

Jesus then told the story of the servant forgiven a great debt who went out and dealt mercilessly with a fellow servant who owed him a debt that was an infinitesimal fraction of what he himself had owed, and who for his mercilessness was utterly condemned. This parable teaches certain lessons which Jesus never tired of teaching.

(1) It teaches that lesson which runs through all the New Testament – we must forgive in order to be forgiven. Those who will not forgive others cannot hope that God will forgive them. 'Blessed are the merciful,' said Jesus, 'for they will receive mercy' (Matthew 5:7). No sooner had Jesus taught his disciples his own prayer than he went on to expand and explain one petition in it: 'For if you forgive others their trespasses, your heavenly Father will also forgive you; but if you do not forgive others, neither will your Father forgive your trespasses' (Matthew 6:14–15). As James had it: 'For judgment will be without mercy to anyone who has shown no mercy' (James 2:13). Divine and human forgiveness go hand in hand.

(2) Why should that be so? One of the great points in this parable is the contrast between the two debts.

The first servant owed his master 10,000 talents – and a talent was the equivalent of fifteen years' wages. That is an incredible debt. It was more than the total budget of the ordinary province. The total revenue of the province which contained Idumaea, Judaea and Samaria was only 600 talents; the total revenue of even a wealthy province like Galilee was only 300 talents. Against that background, this debt is staggering. It was this that the servant was forgiven.

The debt which a fellow servant owed him was a trifling thing; it was 100 denarii, and a denarius was the usual day's wage for a working man. It was therefore a mere fraction of his own debt.

The biblical scholar A. R. S. Kennedy drew this vivid picture to contrast the debts. Suppose they were paid in small coins (he suggested sixpences; we might think in terms of 5-pence pieces or dimes). The 100-denarii debt could be carried in one pocket. The 10,000-talent debt would take an army of about 8,600 carriers to carry it, each carrying a sack of coins 60 lb in weight; and they would form, at a distance of a yard apart, a line five miles long! The contrast between the debts is staggering. The point is that nothing that others can do to us can in any way compare with what we have done to God; and if God has forgiven us the debt we owe to him, we must forgive our neighbours the debts they owe to us. Nothing that we have to forgive can even faintly or remotely compare with what we have been forgiven. As A. M. Toplady's great hymn 'Rock of Ages' has it:

> *Not the labours of my hands*
> *Can fulfil thy law's demands;*
> *Could my zeal no respite know,*
> *Could my tears for ever flow,*
> *All for sin could not atone.*

We have been forgiven a debt which is beyond all paying – for human sin brought about the death of God's own Son – and if that is so, we must forgive others as God has forgiven us, or we can hope to find no mercy.

The unanswerable argument

Mark 2:7–12

Some of the experts in the law were sitting there, and they were debating within themselves, 'How can this fellow speak like this? He is insulting God. Who can forgive sins except one person – God?' Jesus immediately knew in his spirit that this debate was going on in their minds, so he said to them, 'Why do you debate thus in your minds? Which is easier – to say to the paralysed man, "Your sins are forgiven," or to say, "Get up, and lift your bed, and walk around"? Just to let you see that the Son of Man has authority on earth to forgive sins' – he said to the paralysed man – 'I say to you, "Get up! Lift your bed! And go away home!"' And he raised himself, and immediately he lifted his bed, and went out in front of them all. The result was that they were all astonished, and they kept on praising God. 'Never', they kept repeating, 'have we seen anything like this.'

JESUS had attracted the crowds. Because of that, he had attracted the notice of the official leaders of the Jews. The Sanhedrin was their supreme court. One of its great functions was to be the guardian of orthodoxy. For instance, it was the Sanhedrin's duty to deal with anyone who was a false prophet. It seems that it had sent out a kind of scouting party to check up on Jesus; and they were there in Capernaum. No doubt they had taken up a prominent place in the front of the crowd and were sitting there critically watching everything that was going on.

When they heard Jesus say to the man that his sins were forgiven, it came as a shattering shock. It was an essential of Judaism that only God could forgive sins. For any human being to claim to do so was to insult God; that was blasphemy, and the penalty for blasphemy was death by stoning (Leviticus 24:16). At the moment they were not ready to launch their attack in public, but it was not difficult for Jesus to see how their minds were working. So he determined to fling down a challenge and to meet them on their own ground.

It was their own firm belief that sin and sickness were indissolubly linked together. Those who were sick had sinned. So Jesus asked them: 'Is it easier to say to this man, "Your sins are forgiven," or to say, "Get up and walk"?' Any charlatan could say, 'Your sins are forgiven.' There was no possibility of ever demonstrating whether his words were effective or not; such a statement was completely uncheckable. But to say, 'Get up and walk' was to say something whose effectiveness would either be proved or disproved there and then. So Jesus said in effect: 'You say that I have no right to forgive sins? You hold as a matter of belief that if this man is ill he is a sinner and he cannot be cured till he is forgiven? Very well, then, watch this!' So Jesus spoke the word and the man was cured.

The experts in the law were caught at their own game. On their own stated beliefs the man could not be cured, unless he was forgiven. He *was* cured, therefore he *was* forgiven. Therefore, Jesus' claim to forgive sin *must* be true. Jesus must have left a completely baffled set of legal experts; and, worse, he must have left them in a baffled rage. Here was something that must be dealt with: if this went on, all orthodox religion would be shattered and destroyed. In this incident Jesus signed his own death warrant – and he knew it.

For all that, it is an extremely difficult incident. What does it mean that Jesus can forgive sin? There are three possible ways of looking at this.

(1) We could take it that Jesus was *conveying* God's forgiveness to the man. After David had sinned and Nathan had rebuked him into terror and David had humbly confessed his sin, Nathan said: 'The Lord has put away your sin; you shall not die' (2 Samuel 12:13). Nathan was not forgiving David's sin, but he was conveying God's forgiveness to David and assuring him of it. So we could say that what Jesus was doing was that he was assuring the man of God's forgiveness, conveying to him something which God had already given him. That is certainly true, but it does not read as if it was the whole truth.

(2) We could take it that Jesus was acting as God's representative. John says: 'The Father judges no one but has given all judgment to the Son' (John 5:22). If judgment is committed to Jesus, then so must forgiveness be. Let us take a human analogy. Analogies are always imperfect, but we can think only in human terms. We may give another person *power of attorney*; that means to say that we have given that person the absolute disposal of our goods and property. We agree that the other person should act for us, and that that person's actions should be regarded precisely as our own. We could take it that that is what God did with Jesus, that he delegated to him his powers and privileges, and that the word Jesus spoke was none other than the word of God.

(3) We could take it in still another way. The whole essence of Jesus' life is that in him we see clearly displayed the attitude of God to men and women. Now that attitude was the very reverse of the way God's attitude had been perceived. It was not an attitude of stern, severe, austere justice, not an attitude of continual demand. It was an attitude of perfect love, of a heart yearning with love and eager to forgive. Again let us use a human analogy. Lewis Hind in one of his essays tells us of the day that he discovered his father. He had always respected and admired his father; but he had always been more than a little afraid of him. He was in church with his father one Sunday. It was a hot drowsy day. He grew sleepier and sleepier. He could not keep his eyes open as the waves of sleep engulfed him. His head nodded. He saw his father's arm go up; and he was sure that his father was going to shake or strike him. Then he saw his father smile gently and put his arm round his shoulder. He cuddled the boy to himself so that he might rest the more comfortably and held him close with the clasp of love. That day, Lewis Hind discovered that his father was not as he had thought him to be and that his father loved him. That is what Jesus did for humanity and for God. He literally brought men and women God's forgiveness upon earth. Without him, they would never have even remotely known about it. 'I tell you,' he said to the man, 'and I tell you here and now, upon earth, you are a forgiven man.' Jesus showed perfectly the attitude of God to all people. He could say, 'I forgive,' because in him God was saying, 'I forgive.'

The laws of prayer

Mark 11:22–6

Jesus answered, 'Have faith in God. This is the truth I tell you – whoever will say to this mountain, "Be lifted up and be cast into the sea," and who in his heart does not doubt, but believes that what he says is happening, it will be done for him. So then I tell you, believe that you have received everything for which you pray and ask, and it will be done for you. And whenever you stand praying, if you have anything against anyone, forgive it, so that your Father who is in heaven may forgive you your trespasses.'

THIS passage gives us three rules for prayer.

(1) It must be the prayer of faith. The phrase about removing mountains was a quite common Jewish phrase. It was a regular, vivid phrase for *removing difficulties*. It was specially used of wise teachers. A good teacher who could remove the difficulties which the minds of his scholars encountered was called *a mountain-remover.* One who heard a famous Rabbi teach said that 'he saw Resh Lachish as if he were *plucking up mountains*'. So the phrase means that if we have real faith, prayer is a power which can solve any problem and make us able to deal with any difficulty. That sounds very simple, but it involves two things.

First, it involves that we should be willing to take our problems and our difficulties to God. That in itself is a very real test. Sometimes our problems are that we wish to obtain something we should not desire at all, that we wish to find a way to do something we should not even think of doing, that we wish to justify ourselves for doing something to which we should never lay our hands or apply our minds. One of the greatest tests of any problem is simply to say, 'Can I take it to God and can I ask his help?' Second, it involves that we should be ready to accept God's guidance when he gives it. It is the commonest thing in the world for people to ask for advice when all they really want is approval for some action that they are already determined to take. It is useless to go to God and to ask for his guidance unless we are willing to be obedient enough to accept it. But if we do take our problems to God and are humble enough and brave enough to accept his guidance, there does come the power which can conquer the difficulties of thought and of action.

(2) It must be the prayer of expectation. It is the universal fact that anything tried in the spirit of confident expectation has a more than double chance of success. The patient who goes to a doctor and has no confidence in the prescribed remedies has far less chance of recovery than the patient who is confident that the doctor can provide a cure. When we pray, it must never be a mere formality. It must never be a ritual without hope.

⌜A scene from Leonard Merrick's book, *Conrad in Quest of His Youth*, provides a good illustration: "'Do you think prayers are ever answered?' inquired Conrad. "In my life I have sent up many prayers, and always with the attempt to persuade myself that some former prayer had been fulfilled. But I knew. I knew in my heart none ever had been. Things that I wanted have come to me, but – I say it with all reverence

– too late ..." Mr Irquetson's fine hand wandered across his brow. "Once," he began conversationally, "I was passing with a friend through Grosvenor Street. It was when in the spring the tenant's fancy lightly turns to coats of paint, and we came to a ladder leaning against a house that was being redecorated. In stepping to the outer side of it my friend lifted his hat to it. You may know the superstition. He was a university man, a man of considerable attainments. I said, 'Is it possible you believe in that nonsense?' He said, 'N-no, I don't exactly believe in it, but I never throw away a chance'." Suddenly the vicar's inflexion changed, his utterance was solemn, stirring, devout, "I think, sir, that most people pray on my friend's principle – they don't believe in it, but they never throw away a chance.'"

There is much truth in that. For many people prayer is either a pious ritual or a forlorn hope. It should be a thing of burning expectation. Maybe our trouble is that what we want from God is *our* answer, and we do not recognize *his* answer when it comes.

(3) It must be the prayer of charity. The prayers of bitter people cannot penetrate the wall of their own bitterness. Why? If we are to speak with God there must be some bond between us and God. There can never be any intimacy between two people who have nothing in common. The principle of God is love, for he *is* love. If the ruling principle of our hearts is bitterness, we have erected a barrier between ourselves and God. In such circumstances, if our prayers are to be answered we must first ask God to cleanse our hearts from the bitter spirit and put into them the spirit of love. Then we can speak to God and God can speak to us.

The golden rule

> *Jesus said, 'But to you who are listening I say, Love your enemies, do good to those who hate you, bless those who curse you, pray for those who ill-use you. To him who strikes you on one cheek offer the other cheek also. If anyone takes away your cloak, do not stop him taking your tunic, too. Give to everyone who asks you; if anyone takes away your belongings, do not demand them back again. As you would like men to act towards you, so do you act towards them. If you love those who love you, what special grace is there in that? Even sinners love those who love them. If you are kind to those who are kind to you, what special grace is there in that? Even sinners do that. If you lend to those from whom you wish to get, what special grace is in that? Even sinners lend to sinners in order to get as much back again. But you must love your enemies; and do good to them; and lend with no hope of getting anything in return. Your reward will be great and you will be the sons of the Most High, because he is kind both to the thankless and to the wicked. Be merciful as your Father in heaven is merciful; do not judge and you will not be judged; do not condemn and you will not be condemned; forgive and you will be forgiven. Give and it will be given to you.'*

THERE is no commandment of Jesus which has caused so much discussion and debate as the commandment to love our enemies. Before we can obey it we must discover what it means. In Greek there are three words for 'to love'. There is *eran*, which describes passionate love, the love between the sexes. There is *philein*, which describes our love for our nearest and dearest, the warm affection of the heart. Neither of these two words is used here; the word used here is *agapan*, which needs a whole paragraph to translate it.

Agapan describes an active feeling of benevolence towards other people; it means that no matter what others do to us we will never allow ourselves to desire anything but their highest good; and we will deliberately and of set purpose go out of our way to be good and kind to them. This is most suggestive. We cannot love our enemies as we love our nearest and dearest. To do so would be unnatural, impossible and even wrong. But we can see to it that, no matter what others do to us, even if they insult, ill-treat and injure us, we will seek nothing but their highest good.

One thing emerges from this. The love we bear to our dear ones is something we cannot help. We speak of *falling* in love; it is something which happens to us. But this love towards our enemies is not only something of the heart; it is something of the will. It is something which by the grace of Christ we may will ourselves to do.

This passage has in it two great facts about the Christian ethic.

(1) The Christian ethic is *positive*. It does not consist in *not doing* things but in *doing* them. Jesus gave us the Golden Rule which bids us do to others as we would have them do to us. That rule exists in many writers of many creeds in its *negative* form. Hillel, one of the great Jewish Rabbis, was asked by a man to teach him the whole law while he stood

on one leg. He answered, 'What is hateful to thee, do not to another. That is the whole law and all else is explanation.' Philo, the great Jew of Alexandria, said, 'What you hate to suffer, do not do to anyone else.' Isocrates, the Greek orator, said, 'What things make you angry when you suffer them at the hands of others, do not you do to other people.' The Stoics had as one of their basic rules, 'What you do not wish to be done to yourself, do not you do to any other.' When Confucius was asked, 'Is there one word which may serve as a rule of practice for all one's life?' he answered, 'Is not reciprocity such a word? What you do not want done to yourself, do not do to others.'

Every one of these forms is negative. It is not unduly difficult to keep yourself from such action; but it is a very different thing to go out of your way to do to others what you would want them to do to you. The very essence of Christian conduct is that it consists, not in refraining from bad things, but in actively doing good things.

(2) The Christian ethic is based on *the extra thing.* Jesus described the common ways of sensible conduct and then dismissed them with the question, 'What special grace is in that?' So often people claim to be just as good as their neighbours. Very likely they are. But the question of Jesus is, 'How much *better* are you than the ordinary person?' It is not our neighbour with whom we must compare ourselves; we may well stand that comparison very adequately; it is *God* with whom we must compare ourselves; and in that comparison we are all in default.

(3) What is the reason for this Christian conduct? The reason is that it makes us like God, for that is the way he acts. God sends his rain on the just and the unjust. He is

kind to the person who brings him joy and equally kind to the person who grieves his heart. God's love embraces saint and sinner alike. It is that love we must copy; if we, too, seek even our enemy's highest good we will in truth be the children of God.

A sinner's love

Luke 7:36–50

One of the Pharisees invited Jesus to eat with him. He went into the Pharisee's house and reclined at table; and – look you – there was a woman in the town, a bad woman. She knew that he was at table in the Pharisee's house, so she took an alabaster phial of perfume and stood behind him, beside his feet, weeping. She began to wash his feet with tears, and she wiped them with the hairs of her head; and she kept kissing his feet and anointing them with the perfume. When the Pharisee, who had invited him, saw this, he said to himself, 'If this fellow was a prophet, he would have known who and what kind of a person this woman is who keeps touching him, for she is a bad woman.' Jesus answered him. 'Simon, I have something to say to you.' He said, 'Master, say it.' Jesus said, 'There were two men who were in debt to a certain lender. The one owed him 500 denarii, the other 50 denarii. Since they were unable to pay he cancelled the debt to both. Who then will love him the more?' Simon answered, 'I presume, he to whom the greater favour was shown.' He said to him, 'Your judgment is correct.' He turned to the woman and said to Simon, 'Do you see this woman? I came into your house – you gave me no water for my feet. She has washed my feet with her tears, and wiped them with the hairs of her head. You did not give me any kiss. But she, from the time I

22

*came in, has not ceased to kiss my feet. You did not anoint
my head with oil. She has anointed my feet with perfume.
Wherefore, I tell you, her sins – her many sins – are forgiven
for she loved much. He to whom little is forgiven loves little.'
He said to her, 'Your sins are forgiven.' Those who were at
table with him began to say to themselves, 'Who is this who
forgives even sins?' He said to the woman, 'Your faith has
saved you. Go in peace.'*

THIS story is so vivid that it makes one believe that Luke may
well have been an artist.

(1) The scene is the courtyard of the house of Simon the
Pharisee. The houses of well-to-do people were built round
an open courtyard in the form of a hollow square. Often
in the courtyard there would be a garden and a fountain;
and there in the warm weather meals were eaten. It was the
custom that when a Rabbi was at a meal in such a house, all
kinds of people came in – they were quite free to do so – to
listen to the pearls of wisdom which fell from his lips. That
explains the presence of the woman.

When a guest entered such a house three things were
always done. The host placed his hand on the guest's shoulder
and gave him the kiss of peace. That was a mark of respect
which was never omitted in the case of a distinguished Rabbi.
The roads were only dust tracks, and shoes were merely soles
held in place by straps across the foot. So always cool water
was poured over the guest's feet to cleanse and comfort them.
Either a pinch of sweet-smelling incense was burned or a
drop of attar of roses was placed on the guest's head. These
things good manners demanded, and in this case not one of
them was done.

In the middle east the guests did not sit, but reclined, at table. They lay on low couches, resting on the left elbow, leaving the right arm free, with the feet stretched out behind; and during the meal the sandals were taken off. That explains how the woman was standing beside Jesus' feet.

(2) Simon was a Pharisee, one of the separated ones. Why should such a man invite Jesus to his house at all? There are three possible reasons.

(a) It is just possible that he was an admirer and a sympathizer, for not all the Pharisees were Jesus' enemies (cf. Luke 13:31). But the whole atmosphere of discourtesy makes that unlikely.

(b) It could be that Simon had invited Jesus with the deliberate intention of enticing him into some word or action which might have been made the basis of a charge against him. Simon may have been an *agent provocateur.* Again it is not likely, because in verse 40 Simon gives Jesus the title, Rabbi.

(c) Most likely, Simon was a collector of celebrities; and with a half-patronizing contempt he had invited this startling young Galilaean to have a meal with him. That would best explain the strange combination of a certain respect with the omission of the usual courtesies. Simon was a man who tried to patronize Jesus.

(3) The woman was a bad woman, and a notoriously bad woman, a prostitute. No doubt she had listened to Jesus speak from the edge of the crowd and had glimpsed in him the hand which could lift her from the mire of her ways. Round her neck she wore, like all Jewish women, a little phial of concentrated perfume; these were called alabasters, and they were very costly. She wished to pour it on his feet,

for it was all she had to offer. But as she saw him the tears came and fell upon his feet. For a Jewish woman to appear with hair unbound was an act of the gravest immodesty. On her wedding day a girl bound up her hair and never would she appear with it unbound again. The fact that this woman loosed her long hair in public showed how she had forgotten everyone except Jesus.

The story demonstrates a contrast between two attitudes of mind and heart.

(1) Simon was conscious of no need and therefore felt no love, and so received no forgiveness. Simon's impression of himself was that he was a good man in the sight of others and of God.

(2) The woman was conscious of nothing else than a burning need, and therefore was overwhelmed with love for him who could supply it, and so received forgiveness.

The one thing which shuts us off from God is self-sufficiency. And the strange thing is that the better we are, the more keenly we feel our sin. Paul could speak of sinners 'of whom I am the foremost' (1 Timothy 1:15). Francis of Assisi could say, 'There is nowhere a more wretched and a more miserable sinner than I.' It is true to say that the greatest of sins is to be conscious of no sin; but a sense of need will open the door to the forgiveness of God, because God is love, and love's greatest glory is to be needed.

There they crucified him

Luke 23:32–8

Two others who were criminals were brought to be put to death with Jesus. When they came to the place which is called the place of a skull, there they crucified him, and the two criminals, one on his right hand, and one on his left. And Jesus said, 'Father, forgive them, for they do not know what they are doing.' And, as they divided his garments, they cast lots for them. The people stood watching, and the rulers gibed at him. 'He saved others,' they said. 'Let him save himself if he really is the Anointed One of God, the chosen one.' The soldiers also mocked him, coming and offering vinegar to him, and saying, 'If you are the King of the Jews save yourself.' There was also an inscription over him, 'This is the King of the Jews'.

WHEN a criminal reached the place of crucifixion, his cross was laid flat upon the ground. Usually it was a cross shaped like a T with no top piece against which the head could rest. It was quite low, so that the criminal's feet were only two or three feet above the ground. There was a company of pious women in Jerusalem who made it their practice always to go to crucifixions and to give the victim a drink of drugged wine which would deaden the terrible pain. That drink was offered to Jesus and he refused it (Matthew 27:34). He was determined to face death at its worst, with a clear mind and senses unclouded. The victim's arms were stretched out upon the crossbar, and it was usual for the nails to be driven through the wrists. The feet were not nailed, but only loosely bound to the cross. Half-way up the cross there was a projecting piece of wood, called the saddle, which took the weight of the criminal, for otherwise the nails would have torn through his wrists. Then the cross was lifted and set upright in its socket. The terror of crucifixion was this – the pain of that process was terrible but it was not enough to kill, and the victim was left to die of hunger and thirst beneath the blazing noontide sun and the frosts of the night. Many a criminal was known to have hung for a week upon his cross until he died raving mad.

The clothes of the criminal were given as a 'perk' to the four soldiers among whom he marched to the cross. Every Jew wore five articles of apparel – the inner tunic, the outer robe, the girdle, the sandals and the turban. Four were divided among the four soldiers. There remained the great outer robe. It was woven in one piece without a seam (John 19:23–4). To have cut it up and divided it would have ruined it; and so the soldiers gambled for it in the shadow of the cross. It was nothing to them that another criminal was slowly dying in agony.

The inscription set upon the cross was the same placard as was carried before a man as he marched through the streets to the place of crucifixion.

Jesus said many wonderful things, but rarely anything more wonderful than, 'Father, forgive them, for they know not what they do.' Christian forgiveness is an amazing thing. When Stephen was being stoned to death he too prayed, 'Lord, do not hold this sin against them' (Acts 7:60). There is nothing so lovely and nothing so rare as Christian forgiveness.

When the unforgiving spirit is threatening to turn our hearts to bitterness, let us hear again our Lord asking forgiveness for those who crucified him and his servant Paul saying to his friends, 'Be kind to one another, tenderhearted, forgiving one another, as God in Christ has forgiven you' (Ephesians 4:32).

The idea that this terrible thing was done in ignorance runs through the New Testament. Peter later said to the people, 'I know that you acted in ignorance' (Acts 3:17). Paul said that they crucified Jesus because they did not know him (Acts 13:27). Marcus Aurelius, the great Roman emperor and Stoic saint, used to say to himself every morning, 'Today you will meet all kinds of unpleasant people; they will hurt you, and injure you, and insult you; but you cannot live like that; you know better, for you are a man in whom the spirit of God dwells.' Others may have in their hearts the unforgiving spirit, others may sin in ignorance; but we know better. We are Christ's men and women; and we must forgive as he forgave.

The commission of Christ

John 20:19–23

Late on that day, the first day of the week, when for fear of the Jews the doors had been locked in the place where the disciples were, Jesus came and stood in the midst of them, and said: 'Peace be to you.' And when he had said this he showed them his hands and his side. So the disciples rejoiced because they had seen the Lord. Jesus again said to them: 'Peace to you. Even as the Father sent me, so I send you.' When he had said this, he breathed on them and said to them: 'Receive the Holy Spirit. If you remit the sins of any, they are remitted; if you retain them they are retained.'

IT is most likely that the disciples continued to meet in the upper room where the Last Supper had been held. But they met in something very like terror. They knew the intense bitterness of the Jews who had brought about the death of Jesus, and they were afraid that their turn would come next. So they were meeting in terror, listening fearfully for every step on the stair and for every knock at the door, lest the representatives of the Sanhedrin should come to arrest them too. As they sat there, Jesus was suddenly in their midst. He gave them the normal everyday middle-eastern greeting: 'Peace be to you.' It means far more than: 'May you be saved from trouble.' It means: 'May God give you every good thing.' Then Jesus gave the disciples the commission which the Church must never forget.

(1) He said that as God had sent him forth, so he sent them forth. Here is what the New Testament scholar B. F. Westcott called 'The Charter of the Church'. It means three things.

(a) It means that Jesus Christ needs the Church, which is exactly what Paul meant when he called the Church 'the body of Christ' (Ephesians 1:23; 1 Corinthians 12:12). Jesus had come with a message for all people, and now he was going back to his Father. His message could never be taken to all men and women, unless the Church took it. The Church was to be a mouth to speak for Jesus, feet to run upon his errands, hands to do his work. Therefore, the first thing this means is that *Jesus is dependent on his Church*.

(b) It means that the Church needs Jesus. People who are to be sent out need someone to send them; they need a message to take; they need a power and an authority to back the message; they need someone to whom they may turn when they are in doubt and in difficulty. Without Jesus, the Church has no message; without him it has no power; without him it has no one to turn to when up against it; without him it has nothing to enlighten its mind, to strengthen its arm and to encourage its heart. This means that *the Church is dependent on Jesus*.

(c) There remains still another thing. The sending out of the Church by Jesus is parallel to the sending out of Jesus by God. But no one can read the story of the Fourth Gospel without seeing that the relationship between Jesus and God was continually dependent on Jesus' perfect obedience and perfect love. Jesus could be God's messenger only because he rendered to God that perfect obedience and love. It follows that the Church is fit to be the messenger and the instrument of Christ only when it perfectly loves him and perfectly obeys him. The Church must never be out to propagate *its own* message; it must be out to propagate the message of Christ. It must never be out to follow policies of human devising; it must be out to follow the will of Christ. The Church fails whenever it tries to solve some problem in its own wisdom and strength, and leaves out of account the will and guidance of Jesus Christ.

(2) Jesus breathed on his disciples and gave them the Holy Spirit. There is no doubt that, when John spoke in this way, he was thinking back to the old story of the creation. There the writer says: 'Then the Lord God formed man from the dust of the ground, and breathed into his nostrils the breath of life; and the man became a living being' (Genesis 2:7). This was the same picture as Ezekiel saw in the valley of dead, dry bones, when he heard God say to the wind: 'Come from the four winds, O breath, and breathe upon these slain, that they may live' (Ezekiel 37:9). The coming of the Holy Spirit is like the wakening of life from the dead. When he comes upon the Church, it is re-created for its task.

(3) Jesus said to the disciples: 'If you remit the sins of anyone, they are remitted; if you retain them, they are retained.' This is a saying whose true meaning we must be careful to understand. One thing is certain – no one can forgive anyone else's sins. But another thing is equally certain – it is the great privilege of the Church to convey the message of God's forgiveness to men and women. Suppose someone brings us a message from another, our assessment of the value of that message will depend on how well the bringer

of the message knows the sender. If someone proposes to interpret another's thought to us, we know that the value of that person's interpretation depends on the closeness they have to the other.

The apostles had the best of all rights to bring Jesus' message to all people, because they knew him best. If they knew that people were really penitent, they could with absolute certainty proclaim to them the forgiveness of Christ. But equally, if they knew that there was no penitence in their hearts or that they were trading on the love and the mercy of God, they could tell them that until their hearts were altered there was no forgiveness for them. This sentence does not mean that the power to forgive sins was ever entrusted to any individual or group; it means that the power to proclaim that forgiveness was so entrusted, along with the power to warn that forgiveness is not open to the impenitent. This sentence lays down the duty of the Church to convey forgiveness to the penitent in heart and to warn the impenitent that they are forfeiting the mercy of God.

The heart of the gospel

Acts 10:34–43

> *So Peter opened his mouth and said: 'In truth I have come*
> *to understand that God has no favourites; but that in every*
> *nation he who fears him and acts righteously is acceptable*
> *to him. As for the word which God sent to the sons of Israel,*
> *telling the good news of peace through Jesus Christ – this is*
> *he who is Lord of all – you all know the affair that happened*
> *all over Judaea, after the baptism which John preached – you*
> *know about Jesus of Nazareth, about how God anointed him*
> *with the Spirit and with power, about how he went about*
> *healing all who were under the sway of the devil because God*
> *was with him; we are witnesses of all he did in the country*
> *of the Jews and in Jerusalem. And they took him and hanged*
> *him on a tree. It was he whom God raised up on the third*
> *day and made him evident, not to all the people but to the*
> *witnesses elected beforehand by God, to us who were with*
> *him and who ate with him and drank with him after he rose*
> *from the dead. And he gave us orders to preach to the people*
> *and to testify that this is he who was set apart by God, to be*
> *the judge of the living and the dead. To him all the prophets*
> *testify – that everyone who believes in him receives forgiveness*
> *of sins through his name.'*

It is clear that we have here only the barest summary of
what Peter said to Cornelius, which makes it all the more

important because it gives us the very essence of the first preaching about Jesus.

(1) Jesus was sent by God and equipped by him with the Spirit and with power. Jesus, therefore, is God's gift to us. Often, we make the mistake of thinking in terms of an angry God who had to be pacified by something a gentle Jesus did. The early preachers never preached that. To them, the very coming of Jesus was due to the love of God.

(2) Jesus exercised a ministry of healing. It was his great desire to banish pain and sorrow from the world.

(3) They crucified him. Once again, for those who can read between the lines, the sheer horror in the crucifixion is stressed. That is what human sin can do.

(4) He rose again. The power which was in Jesus was not to be defeated. It could conquer the worst that people could do, and in the end it could conquer death.

(5) Christian preachers and teachers are witnesses of the resurrection. To them, Jesus is not a figure in a book or about whom they have heard. He is a living presence whom they have met.

(6) The result of all this is forgiveness of sins and a new relationship with God. Through Jesus, the friendship which should always have existed between men and women and God, but which sin interrupted, has dawned upon the world.

The only way to be right with God

Romans 3:19–26

We know that whatever the law says, it says to those who are within the law, and the function of the law is that every mouth should be silenced and that the whole world should be known to be liable to the judgment of God, because no one will ever get into a right relationship with God by doing the works which the law lays down. What does come through the law is a full awareness of sin. But now a way to a right relationship to God lies open before us quite apart from the law, and it is a way attested by the law and the prophets. For a right relationship to God comes through faith in Jesus Christ to all who believe. For there is no distinction, for all have sinned and all fall short of the glory of God, but they are put into a right relationship with God, freely, by his grace, through the deliverance which is wrought by Jesus Christ. God put him forward as one who can win for us forgiveness of our sins through faith in his blood. He did so in order to demonstrate his righteousness because, in the forbearance of God, there had been a passing over of the sins which happened in previous times; and he did so to demonstrate his righteousness in this present age, so that he himself should be just and that he should accept as just the man who believes in Jesus.

HERE again is a passage which is not easy to understand, but which is full of riches when its true meaning is grasped. Let us see if we can penetrate to the basic truth behind it.

The supreme problem of life is: how can we get into a right relationship with God? How can we feel at peace with God? How can we escape the feeling of estrangement and fear in the presence of God? The answer offered by Judaism was: 'You can attain to a right relationship with God by keeping meticulously all that the law lays down.' But to say that is simply to say that there is no possibility of anyone ever attaining to a right relationship with God, for it is not possible to keep every commandment of the law.

What then is the use of the law? It is that it makes people aware of sin. It is only when they know the law and try to satisfy it that people realize they can never satisfy it. The law is designed to show us our own weaknesses and our own sinfulness. Does that mean that we are shut out from God? Far from it, because the way to God is not the way of law, but the way of grace; not the way of works, but the way of faith.

To show what he means, Paul uses three metaphors.

(1) He uses a metaphor from the *law courts* which we call *justification*. This metaphor thinks of an individual as on trial before God. The Greek word which is translated as *to justify* is *dikaioun*. All Greek verbs which end in *-oun* mean not to *make* someone something, but to *treat*, to *reckon*, to *account* that person as something. If an innocent person appears before a judge, then to treat that person as innocent is the same as *acquittal*. But the point about our relationship to God is that we are utterly guilty, and yet God, in his amazing mercy, treats us, reckons us, accounts us as if we were innocent. That is what justification means.

When Paul says that 'God justifies the ungodly', he means that God treats the ungodly as if they had been good men and women. That is what shocked the Jews to the core of their being. To them, to treat bad people as if they were good was the sign of a wicked judge. 'One who justifies the wicked ... [is] an abomination to the Lord' (Proverbs 17:15). 'I will not acquit the guilty' (Exodus 23:7). But Paul says that is precisely what God does.

How can I know that God is like that? I know *because Jesus said so*. He came to tell us that God loves us, bad as we are. He came to tell us that, although we are sinners, we are still dear to God. When we discover that and believe it, *it changes our whole relationship to God*. We are conscious of our sin, but we are no longer in terror and no longer estranged. Penitent and broken-hearted we come to God, like sorry children coming to their father or mother, and we know that the God we come to is love.

That is what *justification by faith in Jesus Christ* means. It means that we are in a right relationship with God because we believe with all our hearts that what Jesus told us about God is true. We are no longer terrorized, strangers from an angry God. We are children, erring children, trusting in their Father's love for forgiveness. *And we could never have found that right relationship with God, if Jesus had not come to live and to die to tell us how wonderfully he loves us*.

(2) Paul uses a metaphor from *sacrifice*. He says of Jesus that God put him forward as one who can win forgiveness for our sins.

The Greek word that Paul uses to describe Jesus is *hilastērion*. This comes from a verb which means *to propitiate*, to appease or atone. It is a verb which has to do with sacrifice. Under the old system, when the law was broken, a sacrifice was brought to God. The aim was that the sacrifice should turn aside the punishment that should fall upon the one who had broken the law. To put it in another way – someone sinned; that sin put that person at once in a wrong relationship with God; to get back into the right relationship, the sacrifice was offered.

But it was human experience that an animal sacrifice failed entirely to do that. 'For you have no delight in sacrifice; if I were to give a burnt-offering, you would not be pleased' (Psalm 51:16). 'With what shall I come before the Lord, and bow myself before God on high? Shall I come before him with burnt-offerings, with calves a year old? Will the Lord be pleased with thousands of rams, with tens of thousands of rivers of oil? Shall I give my firstborn for my transgression, the fruit of my body for the sin of my soul?' (Micah 6:6–7). Instinctively, people felt that, once they had sinned, the paraphernalia of earthly sacrifice could not put matters right.

So, Paul says: 'Jesus Christ, by his life of obedience and his death of love, made the one sacrifice to God which really and truly atones for sin.' He insists that what happened on the cross opens the door back to a right relationship with God, a door which every other sacrifice is powerless to open.

(3) Paul uses a metaphor from *slavery*. He speaks of the *deliverance* brought about through Jesus Christ. The word is *apolutrōsis*. It means a ransoming, a redeeming, a liberating. It means that men and women were in the power of sin, and that Jesus Christ alone could free them from it.

Finally, Paul says of God that he did all this because he is just, and accepts as just all who believe in Jesus. Paul never said a more startling thing than this. The eighteenth-century

German commentator Johann Bengel called it 'the supreme paradox of the gospel'. Think what it means. It means that God is just and accepts the sinner as being just. The natural thing to say would be: 'God is just, and, therefore, condemns the sinner as a criminal.' But here we have the great paradox – God is just, and somehow, in that incredible, miraculous grace that Jesus came to bring, he accepts the sinner not as a criminal but as a son or a daughter whom he still loves.

What is the essence of all this? Where is the difference between it and the old way of the law? The basic difference is this: the way of obedience to the law is concerned with what we can do for ourselves; the way of grace is concerned with what God can do, and has done, for us. Paul is insisting that nothing we can ever do can win for us the forgiveness of God; only what God has done for us can win that; therefore the way to a right relationship with God lies not in a frenzied, desperate, doomed attempt to win acquittal by our performance; it lies in the humble, penitent acceptance of the love and the grace which God offers us in Jesus Christ.

The gifts of God

Ephesians 1:7–8

> *For it is in him that we have a deliverance which cost his life;*
> *in him we have received the forgiveness of sins, which only*
> *the wealth of his grace could give, a grace which he gave us in*
> *abundant supply, and which conferred on us all wisdom and*
> *all sound sense.*

In this short section, we come face to face with three of the
great concepts of the Christian faith.

(1) There is *deliverance*. The word used is *apolutrōsis*. It
comes from the verb *lutroun*, which means to *ransom*. It is
the word used for ransoming someone who is a prisoner
of war or a slave; for freeing someone from the penalty of
death; for God's deliverance of the children of Israel from
their slavery in Egypt; for God's continual rescuing of his
people in the time of their trouble. In every case, the concept
is of delivering individuals from a situation from which they
were powerless to liberate themselves or from a penalty which
they could never have paid.

So, first of all, Paul says that God delivered people from
a situation from which they could never have delivered
themselves. That is precisely what Christianity did for us.
When Christianity came into this world, men and women
were haunted by the sense of their own powerlessness. They

knew the wrongness of the life which they were living and that they were powerless to do anything about it.

The writings of the Stoic philosopher Seneca are full of this kind of feeling of helpless frustration. Human beings, he said, were overwhelmingly conscious of their inefficiency in necessary things. He said of himself that he was a *homo non tolerabilis*, a man not to be tolerated. Human beings, he said with a kind of despair, love their vices and hate them at the same time. What they need, he cried, is a hand let down to lift them up. The greatest thinkers in the Gentile world knew that they were in the grip of something from which they were helpless to deliver themselves. They needed liberation.

It was just that liberation which Jesus Christ brought. It is still true that he can liberate people from helpless slavery to the things which both attract and disgust them. To put it at its simplest, Jesus can still make bad people good.

(2) There is *forgiveness*. The ancient world was obsessed by the sense of sin. It might well be said that the Old Testament is an expansion of the saying: 'it is only the person that sins who shall die' (Ezekiel 18:4). People were conscious of their own guilt and stood in terror of their god or gods. It is sometimes said that the Greeks had no sense of sin. Nothing could be further from the truth. 'Men', said the Greek poet Hesiod, 'delight their souls in cherishing that which is their bane.' All the plays of Aeschylus are founded on one text: 'The doer shall suffer.' Once someone had done an evil thing, Nemesis was on that person's heels; and punishment followed sin as certainly as night followed day. As Shakespeare had it in *Richard III*:

> *My conscience hath a thousand several tongues,*
> *And every tongue brings in a several tale,*
> *And every tale condemns me for a villain.*

If there was one thing which everyone knew, it was the sense of sin and the dread of God. Jesus changed all that. He taught people not of the hate but of the love of God. Because Jesus came into the world, men and women, even in their sin, discovered God's love.

(3) There is *wisdom* and *sound sense*. The two words in Greek are *sophia* and *phronēsis*, and Christ brought both of them to us. This is very interesting. The Greeks wrote a great deal about these two words; anyone who had both was perfectly equipped for life.

Aristotle defined *sophia* as knowledge of the most precious things. Cicero defined it as knowledge of things both human and divine. *Sophia* was a thing of the searching intellect. *Sophia* was the answer to the eternal problems of life and death, God and the world, and time and eternity.

Aristotle defined *phronēsis* as the knowledge of human affairs and of the things in which planning is necessary. Plutarch, the Greek historian and philosopher, defined it as practical knowledge of the things which concern us. The Roman orator Cicero defined it as knowledge of the things which are to be sought and the things which are to be avoided. Plato defined it as the disposition of mind which enables us to judge what things are to be done and what things are not to be done. In other words, *phronēsis* is the sound sense which enables us to meet and to solve the practical problems of everyday life and living,

It is Paul's claim that Jesus brought us *sophia*, the intellectual knowledge which satisfies the mind, and *phronēsis*, the practical knowledge which enables us to handle the day-to-day problems of practical life and living. There is a certain completeness in the Christian character. There is a type of person who is at home in the study, who moves among theological and philosophical problems with an easy familiarity, and who is yet helpless and impractical in the ordinary everyday affairs of life. There is another kind of person who claims to be practical and who is so engaged with the business of living that there is no time to be concerned with the ultimate things. In the light of the gifts of God through Christ, both of these characters are imperfect. Christ brings to us the solution of the problems both of eternity and of the present time.

Triumphant forgiveness

Colossians 2:13–15

> *God made you alive with him, when you were dead in your*
> *sins and were still uncircumcised Gentiles. He forgave you*
> *all your sins, and wiped out the charge-list which set out all*
> *your self-admitted debts, a charge-list which was based on the*
> *ordinances of the law and was in direct opposition to you. He*
> *nailed it to his cross and put it right out of sight. He stripped*
> *the powers and authorities of all their power and publicly put*
> *them to shame, and, through the cross, led them captive in*
> *his triumphal train.*

ALMOST all great teachers have thought in pictures; and
here Paul uses a series of vivid pictures to show what God
in Christ has done for us. The intention is to show that
Christ has done all that can be done and all that need
be done, and that there is no need to bring in any other
intermediaries for our full salvation. There are three main
pictures here.

(1) Men and women were dead in their sins. They had
no more power than the dead either to overcome sin or to
atone for it. Jesus Christ by his work has liberated all people
both from the power and from the consequences of sin. He
has given them a life so new that it can only be said that he
has raised them from the dead. Further, it was the old belief

that only the Jews were dear to God; but this saving power of Christ has come even to the uncircumcised Gentiles. The work of Christ is a work of power, because it put life into those who were as good as dead; it is a work of grace, because it reached out to those who had no reason to expect the benefits of God.

(2) But the picture becomes even more vivid. As the Revised Standard Version has it, Jesus Christ cancelled the bond which stood against us with its legal demands; as we have translated it, he wiped out the charge-list which set out all our self-admitted debts, a charge-list based on the rulings of the law. There are two Greek words here on which the whole picture depends.

(a) The word for *bond* or *charge-list* is *cheirographon*. It literally means an *autograph*; but its technical meaning – a meaning which everyone would understand – was a note of hand signed by a debtor acknowledging his indebtedness. It was almost exactly what we call an IOU. People's sins had piled up a vast list of debts to God, and it could be said that they definitely acknowledged that debt. More than once, the Old Testament shows the children of Israel hearing and accepting the laws of God and calling down curses on themselves should they fail to keep them (Exodus 24:3; Deuteronomy 27:14–26). In the New Testament, we find the picture of the Gentiles as having not the written law of God which the Jews had, but the unwritten law in their hearts and the voice of conscience speaking within (Romans 2:14–15). People were in debt to God because of their sins – and they knew it. There was a self-confessed written accusation against them, a charge-list, which, as it were, they themselves had signed and admitted as accurate.

(b) The word for *wiping out* is the Greek verb *exaleiphein*. To understand that word is to understand the amazing mercy of God. The substance on which ancient documents were written was either papyrus, a kind of paper made of the pith of the bulrush, or vellum, a substance made of the skins of animals. Both were fairly expensive and certainly could not be wasted. Ancient ink had no acid in it; it lay on the surface of the paper and did not, as modern ink usually does, bite into it. Sometimes, to save paper, a scribe used papyrus or vellum that had already been written on. When he did that, he took a sponge and wiped the writing out. Because it was only on the surface of the paper, the ink could be wiped out as if it had never been. God, in his amazing mercy, banished the record of our sins so completely that it was as if it had never been; not a trace remained.

(c) Paul goes on. God took that written accusation and nailed it to the cross of Christ. It used to be said that, in the ancient world, when a law or a regulation was cancelled, it was fastened to a board and a nail was driven right through it. But it is doubtful if that was the case and if that is the picture here. Rather, it is this – on the cross of Christ, the charge that was against us was itself crucified. It was executed and put completely out of the way, so that it might never be seen again. Paul seems to have searched human activity to find a series of pictures which would show how utterly God in his mercy destroyed the condemnation that was against us.

Here indeed is grace. And that new era of grace is further underlined in another rather obscure phrase. The charge-list had been *based on the ordinances of the law*. Before Christ came, people were under law, and they broke it because no one can keep it perfectly. But now, law is banished and grace has come. We are no longer criminals who have broken the law and are at the mercy of God's judgment; we are sons and daughters who were lost and can now come home to be wrapped around with the grace of God.

(3) One other great picture flashes on the screen of Paul's mind. Jesus has stripped the powers and authorities and made them his captives. As we have seen, the ancient world believed in all kinds of angels and in all kinds of elemental spirits. Many of these spirits were out to bring about ruin. It was they who were responsible for such things as demon-possession. They were completely hostile. Jesus conquered them forever. He *stripped* them; the word used is the word for stripping the weapons and the armour from a defeated enemy. Once and for all, Jesus broke their power. He put them to public shame and led them captive in his triumphant procession. The picture is that of the triumph of a Roman general. When a Roman general had won a really notable victory, he was allowed to march his victorious armies through the streets of Rome, and behind him followed the kings and the leaders and the peoples he had defeated. They were openly branded as his spoils. Paul thinks of Jesus as a conqueror enjoying a kind of cosmic triumph, and in his triumphal procession are the powers of evil, beaten forever, for everyone to see.

In these vivid pictures, Paul sets out the total adequacy of the work of Christ. Sin is forgiven and evil is conquered; what more is necessary?

Pleading for a sinner's pardon

2 Corinthians 2:5–11

If anyone has caused grief, it is not I whom he has grieved, but to some extent – not to overstress the situation – all of you. To such a man, the punishment that has been imposed by the majority is sufficient, so that, so far from inflicting severer punishment, you must forgive him and comfort him, lest such a one be engulfed by excess of grief. So then, I urge you, let your decision in regard to him be a decision of love. For, when I wrote to you, my purpose was to test you, to see if you are obedient in all things. Whatever you have forgiven anyone, I too forgive. For what I have forgiven, if I had anything to forgive, I forgave for your sakes, in the presence of Christ, so that we might not be over-reached by Satan, for we well know his intentions.

THIS is a passage which is an echo of trouble and of unhappiness. When Paul had visited Corinth, there had been a ringleader to the opposition. This man had clearly personally insulted Paul, who had insisted that he must be disciplined. The majority of the Corinthians had come to see that his conduct had not only hurt Paul but had injured the good name of the whole Corinthian church. Disciplinary action had been taken, but there were some who felt that it had not been sufficiently severe and who wanted to impose an even greater punishment.

It is now that the supreme greatness of Paul emerges. His plea is that enough has been done; the man is now sorry, and to discipline him further would do far more harm than good. It might simply drive the man to despair, and to do that is not to serve Christ and the Church, but to offer an opportunity for Satan to take hold of the man. Had Paul acted in this way through merely human motives, he would have gloated over the hard fate of his former enemy. Nowhere is the majesty of his character revealed so clearly as on this occasion, when, in the graciousness of his heart, he pleads for mercy on the man who had hurt him so much. Here is a supreme example of Christian conduct in the face of injury and insult.

(1) Paul did not take the matter personally at all. It was not the injury done to his personal feelings that was important. What he was anxious about was the good discipline and the peace of the Church. There are some people who take everything personally. Criticism, even when it is kindly meant and kindly given, is taken as a personal insult. Such people do more than anyone else to disturb the peace of a fellowship. It would be a good thing to remember that criticism and advice are usually offered not to hurt us but to help us.

(2) Paul's motive in taking disciplinary action was not vengeance but correction; he aimed not to knock the man down but to help him to get up. His aim was to judge not by the standards of abstract justice but by the standards of Christian love. The fact is that, quite often, sins are good qualities gone wrong. The person who can plan a successful burglary has initiative and organizing power; pride is a kind of intensification of the independent spirit; meanness is thrift run to seed. Paul's aim in discipline was not to eradicate such

qualities as an individual might have, but rather to harness them to higher purposes. The Christian duty is not to render sinners harmless by battering them into submission, but to inspire them to goodness.

(3) Paul's insistence was that punishment must never drive to despair and must never take the heart out of anyone. The wrong kind of treatment is often the last straw that finally pushes a person into the arms of Satan. Over-severity may well drive people from the Church and its fellowship, while correction introduced in a sympathetic way might well bring them in. The English essayist Charles Lamb had a sister, Mary, who had terrible bouts of insanity, and who was harshly treated by her mother. She used to sigh: 'Why is it that I never seem able to do anything to please my mother?' The founder of the Reformation, Martin Luther, could scarcely bear to pray the Lord's Prayer because his own father had been so stern that the word 'father' painted a picture of grim terror to him. Luther used to say: 'Spare the rod and spoil the child – yes; but beside the rod keep an apple, to give the child when he has done well.' Punishment should encourage and not discourage. In the last analysis, this can happen only when we make it clear that, even when we are carrying out punishment, we still believe in the individual concerned.

The law of liberty and the law of mercy

James 2:12–13

So speak and so act as those who are going to be judged under the law of liberty. For he who acts without mercy will have judgment without mercy. Mercy triumphs over judgment.

JAMES reminds his readers of two great facts of the Christian life.

(1) Christians live under the law of liberty, and it is by the law of liberty that they will be judged. What he means is this. Unlike the Pharisees and the orthodox Jews, Christians are not men and women whose lives are governed by the external pressure of a whole series of rules and regulations imposed on them from outside. They are governed by the inner compulsion of love. They follow the right way, the way of love to God and love to other people, not because any external law compels them to do so nor because any threat of punishment frightens them into doing so, but because the love of Christ within their hearts makes them want to do so.

(2) Christians must always remember that only those who show mercy will find mercy. This is a principle which runs through all Scripture. Ben Sirach wrote: 'Forgive your neighbour the wrong he has done, and then your sins will be pardoned when you pray. Does anyone harbour anger

against another, and expect healing from the Lord? If one has no mercy to another like himself, can he then seek pardon for his own sins?' (Sirach 28:2–5). Jesus said: 'Blessed are the merciful, for they will receive mercy' (Matthew 5:7). 'If you forgive others their trespasses, your heavenly Father will also forgive you; but if you do not forgive others, neither will your Father forgive your trespasses' (Matthew 6:14–15). 'Do not judge, so that you may not be judged. For with the judgment you make you will be judged' (Matthew 7:1–2). He tells of the condemnation which fell upon the unforgiving servant, and ends the parable by saying: 'So, my heavenly Father will also do to every one of you, if you do not forgive your brother or sister from your heart' (cf. Matthew 18:23–35).

Scripture teaching is agreed that those who would find mercy must themselves be merciful. And James goes even further, for in the end he says that mercy triumphs over judgment – by which he means that in the day of judgment those who have shown mercy will find that their mercy has even blotted out their own sin.

The sinner's self-deception

1 John 1:8–10

> *If we say that we have no sin, we deceive ourselves, and the truth is not in us. If we confess our sins, we can rely on him in his righteousness to forgive us our sins and to make us clean from all unrighteousness.*
>
> *If we say that we have not sinned, we make him a liar, and his word is not in us.*

IN this passage, John describes and condemns two further mistaken ways of thought.

(1) There are some people who say that they have no sin. That may mean either of two things.

It may describe people who say that they have no responsibility for their sin. It is easy enough to find defences behind which to seek to hide. We may blame our sins on our up-bringing or on our genes, on our environment, on our temperament or on our physical condition. We may claim that someone misled us and that we were led astray. It is a human characteristic that we seek to shuffle out of the responsibility for sin. Or it may describe people who claim that they can sin and come to no harm.

It is John's insistence that, when people have sinned, excuses and self-justifications are irrelevant. The only thing which will meet the situation is humble and penitent confession to God and, if need be, to other people too.

Then John says a surprising thing. He says that we can depend on God *in his righteousness* to forgive us if we confess our sins. On the face of it, we might well have thought that God *in his righteousness* would have been much more likely to condemn than to forgive. But the point is that God, because he is righteous, never breaks his word; and Scripture is full of the promise of mercy to all who come to him with penitent hearts. God has promised that he will never despise the contrite heart and he will not break his word. If we humbly and sorrowfully confess our sins, he will forgive. The very fact of making excuses and looking for self-justification shuts us out from forgiveness, because it blocks our way to penitence; the very fact of humble confession opens the door to forgiveness, for those with penitent hearts can claim the promises of God.

(2) There are some people who say that they have not in fact sinned. That attitude is not nearly so uncommon as we might think. Any number of people do not really believe that they have sinned and rather resent being called sinners. Their mistake is that they think of sin as the kind of thing which gets into the news. They forget that sin is *hamartia*, which literally means a *missing of the target*. To fail to be as good a father, mother, wife, husband, son, daughter, employee or person as we might be is to sin; and that includes us all.

In any event, anyone who claims not to have sinned is in effect doing nothing less than calling God a liar, for God has said that all have sinned.

So, John condemns those who believe that they are so far advanced in knowledge and in the spiritual life that sin for them has ceased to matter; he condemns those who evade the responsibility for their sin or who hold that sin has no effect upon them; he condemns those who have never even realized that they are sinners. The essence of the Christian life is first to realize our sin and then to go to God for that forgiveness which can wipe out the past and for that cleansing which can make the future new.

The sin for which there is no forgiveness

Mark 3:28–30

> 'This is the truth I tell you – all sins will be forgiven to the sons of men – I mean all the insulting things that they say; but whoever insults the Holy Spirit will not be forgiven forever but he has made himself guilty of the sin that not even eternity can wipe out.' This he said because they were saying, 'He has an unclean spirit.'

IF we are to understand what this terrible saying means, we must first understand the circumstances in which it was said. It was said by Jesus when the scribes and Pharisees had declared that the cures he performed were performed not by the power of God, but by the power of the devil. These men had been able to look at the incarnate love of God and to think it the incarnate power of Satan.

We must begin by remembering that Jesus could not have used the phrase 'the Holy Spirit' in the full Christian sense of the term. The Spirit in all his fullness did not come until Jesus had returned to his glory. It was not until Pentecost that there came to men and women the supreme experience of the Holy Spirit. Jesus must have used the term in the *Jewish* sense of the term. Now in Jewish thought the Holy Spirit had two great functions. First, he revealed God's truth; second, he enabled that truth to be recognized. That will give us the key to this passage.

(1) The Holy Spirit enabled men and women to recognize God's truth when it entered their lives. But if people refuse to exercise any God-given faculty they will in the end lose it. If they live in the dark long enough they will lose the ability to see. If they stay in bed long enough they will lose the power to walk. If they refuse to do any serious study they will lose the power to study. And if people refuse the guidance of God's Spirit often enough they will become in the end incapable of recognizing that truth when they see it. In their eyes, evil becomes good and good evil. They can look on the goodness of God and call it the evil of Satan.

(2) Why should such a sin have no forgiveness? The biblical scholar H. B. Swete says, 'To identify the source of good with the embodiment of all evil implies a moral wreck for which the Incarnation itself provides no remedy.' The 1920s Bishop of Derby, A. J. Rawlinson, calls it 'essential wickedness', as if here we see the quintessence of all evil. The Lutheran scholar Johannes Bengel said that all other sins are *human* but this sin is *Satanic*. Why should all this be so?

Consider the effect of Jesus on people. The very first effect is to make them see their own utter unworthiness in comparison with the beauty and the loveliness of the life of Jesus. 'Go away from me, Lord,' said Peter, 'for I am a sinful man!' (Luke 5:8). When the Japanese condemned murderer Tokichi Ishii first read the story of the gospel he said, 'I stopped. I was stabbed to the heart as if pierced by a five-inch nail. Shall I call it the love of Christ? Shall I call it his compassion? I do not know what to call it. I only know that I believed and my hardness of heart was changed.' The first reaction was that he was stabbed to the heart. The result of that sense of unworthiness and the result of that stabbed heart is a heartfelt penitence, and penitence is the only condition of forgiveness. But, if people have got themselves into such a state, by repeated refusals to listen to the promptings of the Holy Spirit, that they cannot see anything lovely in Jesus at all, then the sight of Jesus will not give them any sense of sin; because they have no sense of sin they cannot be penitent, and because they are not penitent they cannot be forgiven.

One of the Lucifer legends tells how one day a priest noticed in his congregation a magnificently handsome young man. After the service, the young man stayed for confession. He confessed so many and such terrible sins that the priest's hair stood on end. 'You must have lived long to have done all that,' the priest said. 'My name is Lucifer and I fell from heaven at the beginning of time,' said the young man. 'Even so,' said the priest, 'say that you are sorry, say that you repent and even you can be forgiven.' The young man looked at the priest for a moment and then turned and strode away. He would not and could not say it; and therefore he had to go on still desolate and still damned.

There is only one condition of forgiveness and that is penitence. As long as people see loveliness in Christ, as long as they hate sin even if they cannot leave it, even if they are in the mud and the mire, they can still be forgiven. But if people, by repeated refusals of God's guidance, have lost the ability to recognize goodness when they see it, if they have got their moral values inverted until evil to them is good and good to them is evil, then, even when they are confronted by Jesus, they are conscious of no sin; they cannot repent and therefore they can never be forgiven. That is the sin against the Holy Spirit.

Books by
WILLIAM BARCLAY

INSIGHTS SERIES

The Lord's Prayer
Christmas
Easter
Money
Prayer
Joy
Parables
Miracles
Forgiveness

THE NEW DAILY STUDY BIBLE

The Gospel of Matthew Vol. 1
The Gospel of Matthew Vol. 2
The Gospel of Mark
The Gospel of Luke
The Gospel of John Vol. 1
The Gospel of John Vol. 2
The Acts of the Apostles
The Letter to the Romans
The Letters to the Corinthians
The Letters to the Galatians and the Ephesians
The Letters to the Philippians, Colossians and Thessalonians
The Letters to Timothy, Titus and Philemon
The Letter to the Hebrews
The Letters to James and Peter
The Letters of John and Jude
The Revelation of John Vol. 1
The Revelation of John Vol. 2

MISCELLANEOUS

A Beginner's Guide to the New Testament
God's Young Church

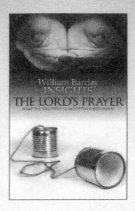

Christmas

What the Bible Tells Us about the Christmas Story

WILLIAM BARCLAY

Foreword by

NICK BAINES

978-0-7152-0858-8 (paperback)

See our website for details.

www.standrewpress.com

SAINT ANDREW PRESS

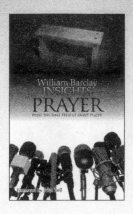